WHAT IS DIWALI?

WRITTEN BY
ANITA MISHRA

FESTIVAL OF LIGHTS

A bright Hindu holiday!

Diwali is a five-day holiday celebrated by Hindu people in India and around the world. It celebrates the victory of good over evil.

During Diwali, people adorn their homes with lots of candles, diyas, and LED bulbs. These shining lights and flames symbolize how light triumphs over darkness.

Other Diwali traditions include creating colorful rangoli patterns, decorating your home with flower garlands, exchanging gifts with loved ones, and sharing all sorts of delicious sweets with family and friends!

WHAT IS A DIYA?
A diya is a traditional clay lamp that burns oil or ghee. People ignite a cotton wick to light it up.

LET'S LEARN MORE ABOUT DIWALI!

WHEN IS DIWALI?

Diwali is celebrated on the Kartik Amavasya night of the Hindu lunar calendar. This is the darkest night of the month.

DID YOU KNOW?
The Hindu lunar calendar is a traditional timekeeping system that uses both lunar and solar cycles to determine dates. It is also known as the lunisolar calendar.

The Hindu calendar is different to the Gregorian calendar, so the dates don't always line up. This means Diwali usually falls sometime in October or November.

Here is how Diwali is written in Hindi:

AMAVASYA
The night of the new moon.

KARTIK
The eighth month of the Hindu lunar calendar.

WHAT'S IN A NAME?

Diwali is the shortened form of the word Deepavali.

The word Deepavali was created by merging "deep" (which means lanterns, candles, or lights) and "aavali" (which means a row or a line).

The term "Deepon ki aavali" refers to the arrangement of diyas or lamps in a line.

THE STORY OF DIWALI

Once upon a time, in the city of Ayodhya (the capital of Kosala), there was a righteous king named Dasharath. He had three wives and four children. Ram, the eldest son, was the beloved crown prince of the kingdom.

But Ram's stepmother Kaikeyi, the third wife of King Dasharath, had different plans. She had saved Dasharath's life in battle, and he had granted her two boons for this. Kaikeyi wanted her own son, Bharath, to inherit the throne of Ayodhya, so she urged Dasharath to honor his promise and grant her these two boons: appointing Bharath as the king, and sending Ram into exile for fourteen years.

With a heavy heart, Dasharath fulfilled his promise and exiled his beloved son for fourteen years. Ram, along with his wife, Sita, and his brother Lakshman, left Ayodhya and went into a forest.

During their exile in the forest of Panchvati, the demoness Surpanakha fell in love with Ram. When Ram refused to marry her, she attacked his wife, Sita, out of jealousy. Lakshman defended Sita and wounded Surpanakha.

In a rage, Surpanakha complained to her brother Ravan, the king of Lanka. To avenge his sister, Ravan summoned a shape-shifting demon and ordered

him to transform into a golden deer and lure Ram and Lakshman away from their hut. Chasing the golden deer, Ram and Lakshman went deep into the forest.

Meanwhile, Ravan disguised himself as a sage and abducted Sita, taking her to Lanka. When the two brothers discovered that Sita had been captured, they immediately set off to bring her back.

During their journey, they came across Hanuman, a vanara (monkey-like creature) and devout worshipper of Ram. Hanuman was the ideal companion, unmatched in loyalty. He had the ability to become as small as a fly or as huge as a mountain.

After an extensive search, Hanuman found Sita and informed the brothers. Ram, Lakshman, Hanuman, and his army of vanaras set out to rescue Sita. In an epic battle, Ram defeated Ravan and freed Sita.

Luckily, the fourteen years of exile had already come to an end, so Ram, Lakshman, and Sita returned to Ayodhya.

It was the new moon night when the trio reached Ayodhya, and the people of Ayodhya had decorated the entire city with glowing diyas to welcome back their beloved prince.

THE FIVE DAYS OF DIWALI

Diwali is celebrated over a five-day period. Each day has its own significance.

DAY 1:
Dhanteras marks the beginning of Diwali

DAY 2:
Choti Diwali is the second day

DAY 3:
Main Diwali and **Laxmi Puja** — this day is the Kartik Amavasya

DAY 4:
Govardhan Puja

DAY 5:
Bhai Dooj marks the last day of Diwali

PUJA
In Hinduism, people refer to the ritual of worship as puja.

DAY 1: DHANTERAS

On this day, people buy new gold or silver ornaments or new utensils. It is believed that buying these things brings home good luck and prosperity. Some families also buy new toys for their children on this day.

Day 2: Choti Diwali

On Choti Diwali, many worship Lord Krishna as they prepare for the next day. People decorate their homes with lights and diyas, and children make colorful rangolis inside or in front of their homes. Most people prepare a wide variety of delicious sweets to offer to God and share with friends and family.

Day 3: Main Diwali

Hooray! It's the main Diwali day. Children light up diyas and lamps and enjoy watching the fireworks with their family and friends. On this day, people also perform puja for Goddess Laxmi, who brings wealth and prosperity. After offering sweets to the goddess, people eat lots and lots of delicious food!

Day 5: Bhai Dooj

Bhai Dooj is celebrated on day 5, and it marks the last day of Diwali. On this day, brothers and sisters express their love for each other. Sisters tie a thread on their brothers' hands, while brothers promise to safeguard their sisters, and give them gifts of their own.

FIREWORKS

Fireworks during Diwali is a fairly new concept. It certainly didn't happen when Ram, Lakshman, and Sita returned home from exile. But over the years, it has become a part of the tradition. It's fun for children to watch the fireworks and also for families and friends to gather together and celebrate.

GREEN DIWALI

Fireworks are pretty, but they can cause air pollution. Some people take care to choose eco-friendly fireworks, and always pick up the debris afterward! You can celebrate without fireworks too, of course! Hang LED lights and use clay diyas and oil lamps to make your family gatherings beautiful!

WHAT IS RANGOLI?

Rangoli is an Indian art form, where colorful patterns are made on the floor — usually from colored flour, sand, rice, or flower petals. On Diwali, people create rangoli in front of their homes to welcome guests, and some make the colorful art in front of their home temples as well.

Rangoli is believed to invite positive energy, wealth, and prosperity. Adding diyas and candles to the pattern turns it into a beautiful Diwali feature!

DID YOU KNOW?
Many schools, colleges, and offices conduct rangoli competitions right before Diwali. May the best artist win!

To learn how to make your own rangoli, turn to the next page!

RANGOLI: STEP-BY-STEP

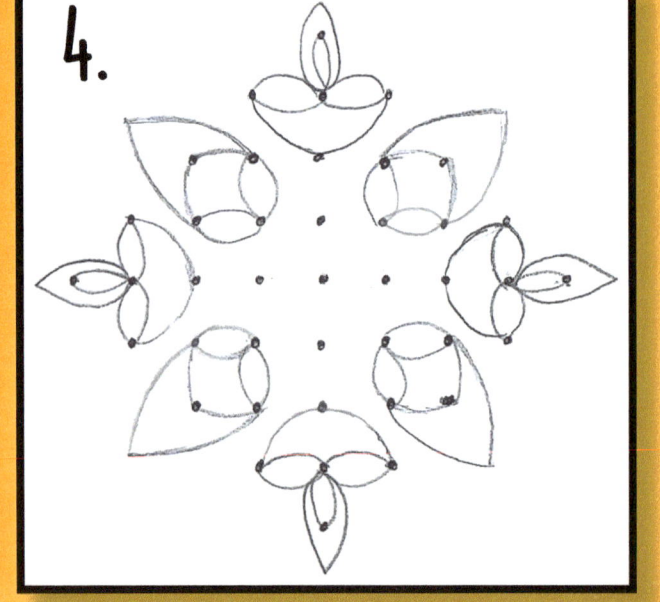

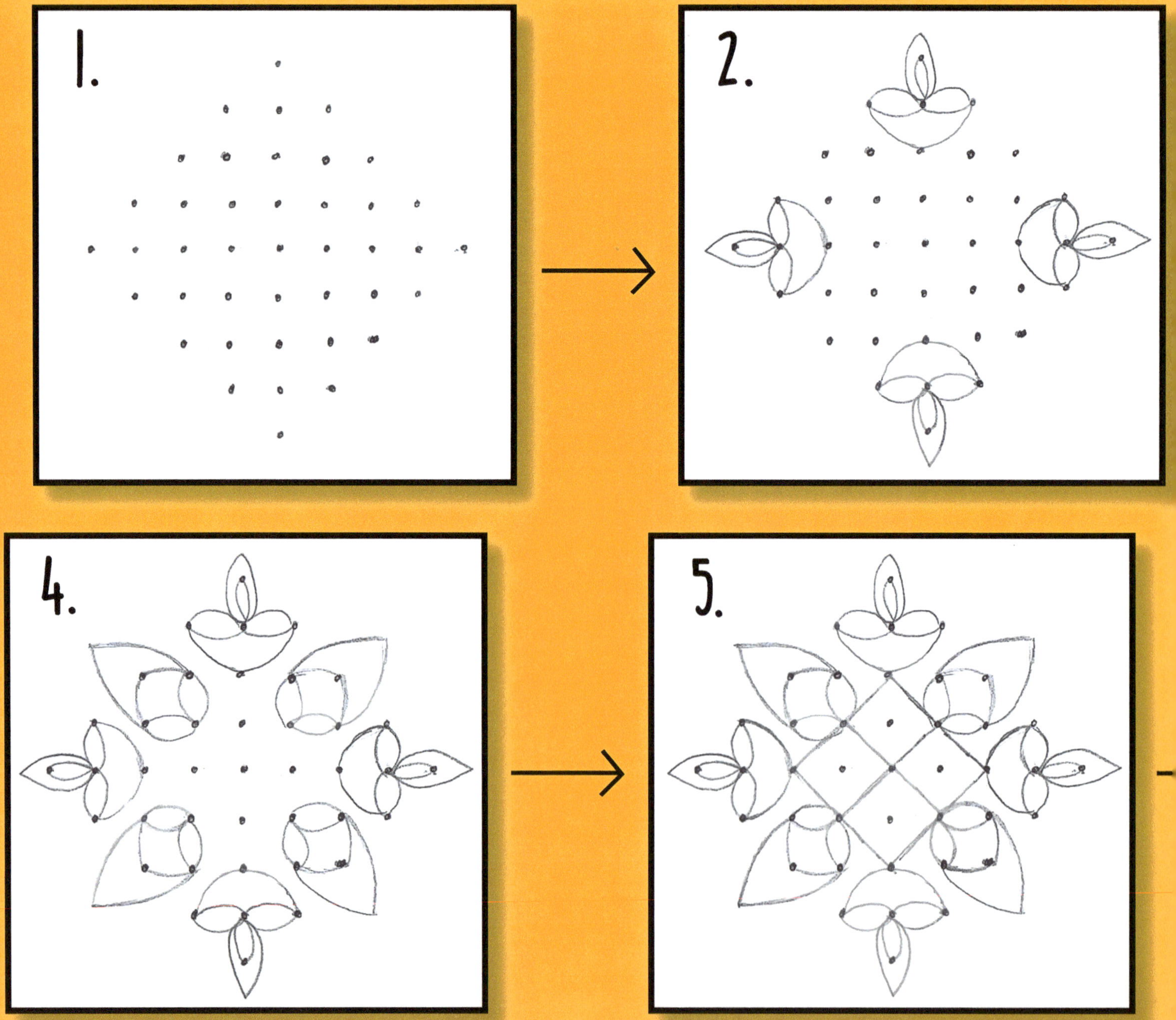

INSTRUCTIONS

- Start with a grid of dots.
- Add patterns, using the dots as a guide. Try to keep your patterns symmetrical.
- Add more and more details until you are happy with the pattern.
- Color or fill your rangoli using bright, bold colors.
- What a beautiful rangoli creation!

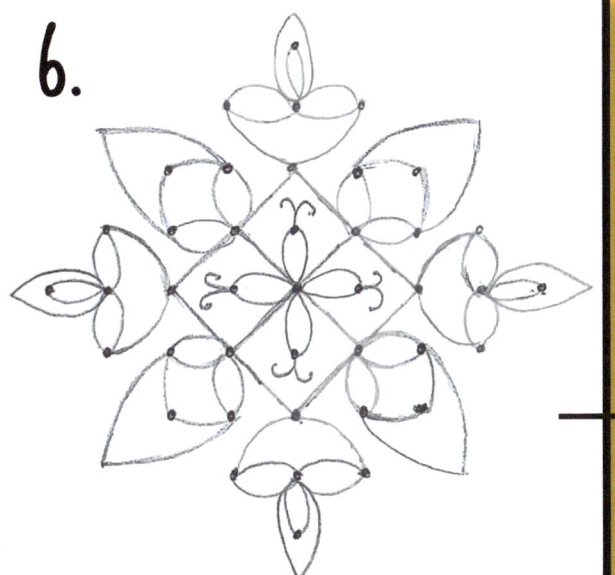

TRADITIONAL DIWALI FOODS

Turn the page to find recipes for two of these delicious treats!

KAJU KATLI

This mildly sweet, nutty dessert is made from powdered cashews, sugar, and water. Once the dough is prepared, they are cut into their signature diamond shape. Learn to make these later in the book!

BESAN KE LADOO

These melt-in-your-mouth sweets are a holiday favorite for many. They are made from roasted gram (chickpea) flour, sugar, and ghee — and some people add cashews to give a nutty flavor.

GULAB JAMUN

These sweets are best eaten warm. To make them, balls of milk-based dough are deep fried and then soaked in cardamom-flavored sugar syrup. Yum!

CHAKLI

Believe it or not, It *is* possible to have too many sweets — which is why Chakli is also popular on Diwali! Made of rice flour and gram flour, this spiral-shaped snack is deep fried for a crispy, savory taste.

LET'S MAKE GULAB JAMUN!

Gulab Jamun is one of the most loved Indian sweets. Balls of dough are fried and then soaked in a sweet syrup.

Syrup ingredients
- 600g sugar
- 850ml water
- 1 tsp cardamom powder

Dough ingredients
- 250g khoya
- 50g all-purpose flour
- ¼ tsp baking powder
- 400–600ml oil for frying

What will you sprinkle on top?

Method

1. In a deep pan, bring the syrup ingredients to a boil.
2. Stir until the sugar dissolves, then remove from the heat and set aside.
3. In a bowl, mix the dough ingredients together into a smooth dough.
4. Break off small handfuls of dough and roll them into smooth balls. You should get around 50 from this recipe!
5. Heat the oil in a deep frying pan. (Ask an adult to help!)
6. Fry the dough balls in batches, carefully turning them over after a few minutes until they are golden. (It will take roughly 7 minutes to fry each batch.)
7. Put the hot, fried balls directly into the sugar syrup.
8. Let the Gulab Jamuns soak in the syrup for three hours.

KHOYA

Khoya is easily available in Indian grocery stores. To make it yourself, boil milk in a non-stick pan. Stir continuously until the water evaporates and soft milk solids are left behind.

LET'S MAKE KAJU KATLI!

Sweet and creamy, these cashew fudge slices are a popular Indian treat!

Ingredients
- 250g cashew nuts
- 100ml water
- 100g sugar

Method
1. Grind cashews into a fine powder using a food processor.
2. Boil water and sugar in a pan until the syrup thickens to one-string consistency.
3. Add the cashew powder to the syrup and simmer until the mixture thickens a little bit more. Stir it the whole time!
4. Pour the mixture onto parchment paper and let it cool for 5-10 minutes.
5. Knead the mixture for 2 minutes until it forms a ball of dough.
6. Roll out the dough so it is about 4mm thick.
7. Cut into diamond-shaped pieces.

TOP TIP! One-string consistency syrup is when the syrup makes one string between your thumb and forefinger.

Kaju katli are often decorated with silver leaf (varka) or powdered sugar.

DIWALI GREETINGS

Now you know about Diwali. If you have Indian friends, here are some ways to wish them Happy Diwali.

"SHUBH DIWALI!"

Pronunciation: *Shub Dih-vahl-ee*
Meaning: "Happy Diwali!"

"DEEPAVALI KI HARDIK SHUBHKAMNAYEIN!"

Pronunciation: *Dee-pa-v'li kee-hardik shub-kahm-nine*
Meaning: "Heartfelt wishes for Diwali!"

AROUND THE WORLD

There are many Indian communities around the world. Let's take a look at how some of them celebrate Diwali!

FIJI
The celebration of Diwali in Fiji is pretty similar to that in India. Houses are decorated with lamps and candles, and the sky is lit up with fireworks. Diwali is even a public holiday in Fiji.

SINGAPORE
Did you know that in Singapore there's a district known as Little India? On Diwali, the streets glow with lights and decorations, just like India. Diwali is celebrated in Little India on a grand scale — with Indian food festivals, street shows, traditional handicrafts, and a decoration market. A fun time to visit Singapore for sure!

MALAYSIA
Although Malaysia is an Islamic country, the main day of Diwali is celebrated as a national holiday.

USA
Diwali fireworks are an annual sight at the BAPS Shri Swaminarayan Mandir in Lilburn, Georgia.

NEPAL
Diwali is celebrated as Tihar for five days in Nepal. For the first four days, a different animal is honored: the crow, the dog, the cow, and finally the ox. Then on day five, Bhai Tika is celebrated just like Bhai Dooj in India.

UK
Diwali celebrations in London and Leicester are considered to be the most significant ones outside of India. In Leicester, the light event is so magical that thousands of tourists visit every year to witness it.

AUSTRALIA
Major Diwali celebrations take place in the cities of Sydney and Melbourne. Melbourne's Federation Square event is particularly famous for its grand display of fireworks.

DIWALI CRAFT IDEAS

PAPER LANTERN

Fold a piece of colored paper in half along the long edge. Cut a slit from the folded side toward the open side, but stop cutting 2.5cm away from the open side. Cut more slits in the same way, 1cm apart, all down the folded edge. Then open the paper and glue the two short edges together. Make a paper handle and stick to the top. Hang your beautiful lanterns wherever you want!

FLOWER GARLANDS AND WALL HANGINGS

String flowers together to create garlands. These look pretty, and they smell good, too! You can also cut out shapes from colored foam or paper, and stick them to string or scraps of lace to create Diwali wall hangings. Hang your decorations at the entrance to your home, bedroom, or classroom.

DECORATED DIYAS

Buy plain clay diyas or craft your own. Then use paint to decorate them in colors of your choice. These make wonderful gifts or pretty decorations to place around your home — or even as part of your rangoli display!

DIWALI CARDS

Design your own Diwali cards for friends and family. Decorate them with stickers and drawings. You can draw traditional Hindu symbols or pictures of things that are associated with Diwali, such as diyas, rangoli patterns, Diwali sweets, and fireworks. Write a meaningful message inside and then deliver the cards on Diwali!

DIWALI GIFT IDEAS

Giving gifts is traditional during Diwali. Even if you don't celebrate this festival, it can be thoughtful to give gifts to those who do. Here are a few ideas. You could even make some of these yourself!

- Handmade Diwali greeting cards
- Assorted sweets gift box
- Assorted nuts gift box
- Decorated diyas
- Scented candles
- Floating candles

Tell Me More!
NEW IDEAS FOR KIDS

First published in Great Britain in 2025
by *Tell Me More!* **Books**

Text copyright ©2025 Anita Mishra
Design copyright ©2025 Shari Black

ISBN: 9781917200325

Picture credits: Thanks to
Adobe Stock, Phive's Images,
and Anita Mishra.

All rights reserved. Without limiting the rights under the copyright reserved above, no part of this publication may be reproduced, stored in, or introduced into a retrieval system, or transmitted, in any form, or by any means (electronic, mechanical, photocopying, recording or otherwise), without the prior written permission of the copyright owner.

WWW.TELLMEMOREBOOKS.COM

LEARN ABOUT OTHER HOLIDAYS AND FESTIVALS

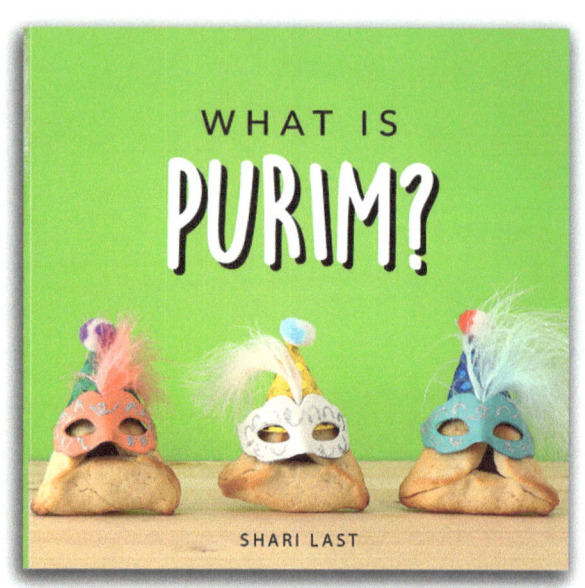

What is Purim?

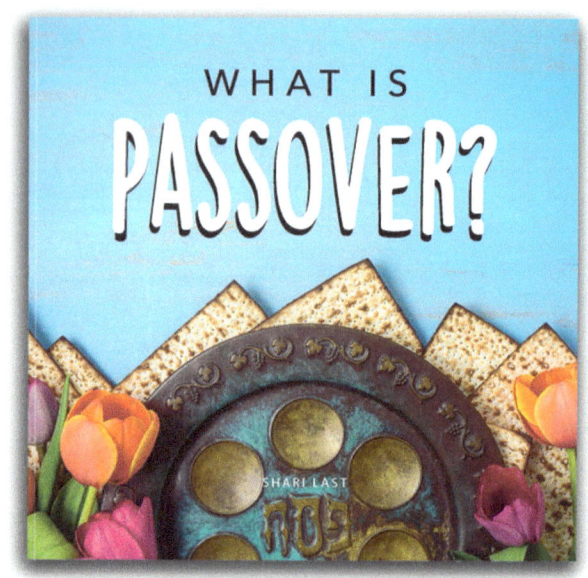

What is Passover?

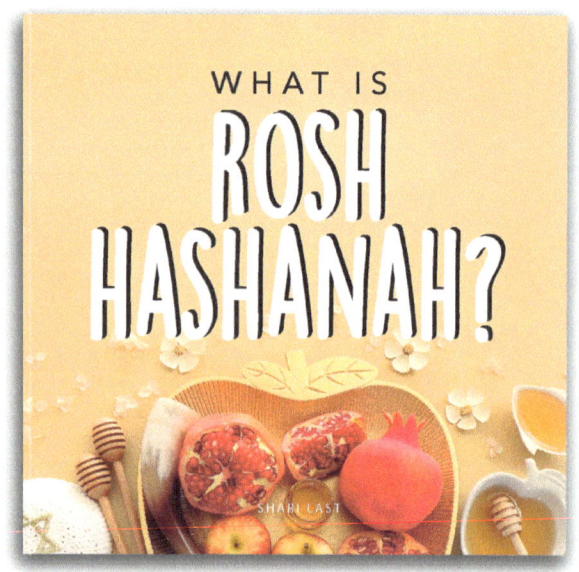

What is Rosh Hashanah?

What is Shavuot?

What is Hanukkah?

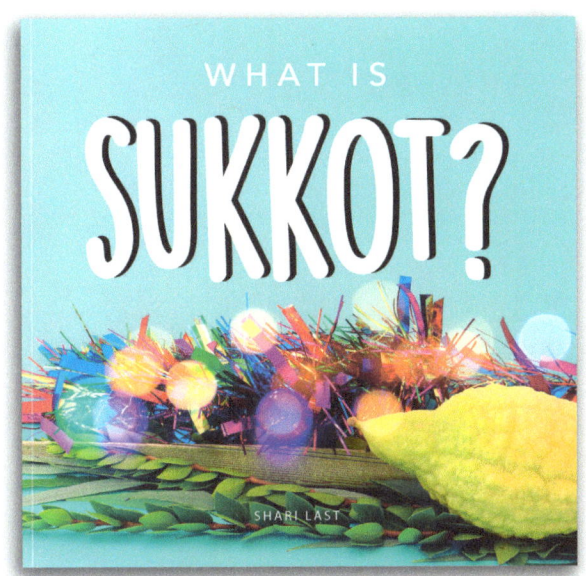

What is Sukkot?

Tell Me More! Books is an independent publishing company that aims to help children explore new ideas through informative, beautiful, and engaging books.

WWW.TELLMEMOREBOOKS.COM

www.ingramcontent.com/pod-product-compliance
Lightning Source LLC
Chambersburg PA
CBHW041118070526
44584CB00002B/206